THE
FIRST CHRISTMAS

THE FIRST CHRISTMAS

Written and illustrated by Carol Heyer

ideals children's books.
Nashville, Tennessee

ISBN-13: 978-0-8249-5566-3

Published by Ideals Children's Books
An imprint of Ideals Publications
A Guideposts Company
Nashville, Tennessee
www.idealsbooks.com

Color separations by Precision Color Graphics, Franklin, Wisconsin

Printed in Italy by LEGO

Library of Congress CIP data on file

10 9 8 7 6 5 4

The illustrations in this book are rendered in acrylic paints and using live models.

*My special thanks to models David Atkinson, William Heyer, Ailsa Hutson,
Cari Sterling, Cecily Vos, and Katherine Zwers.*

Now and always, my work is dedicated to my
parents, William and Merlyn Heyer, for their
unceasing support and encouragement.
—C. H.

🎁 At Christmastime

we think of gifts and Christmas trees. We think of cookies and candies. But most of all, we think of Jesus and remember that Christmas is when we celebrate his birthday.

More than 2,000 years ago, Jesus was born to Mary and Joseph in a town called Bethlehem. This is the story of Jesus' birth.

A young girl named Mary was engaged to Joseph, a carpenter in the city of Nazareth. One day an angel named Gabriel suddenly appeared before the girl.

"Hello, Mary," said Gabriel. "Do not be afraid. I come from God. He has chosen you to carry his son. The baby's name will be Jesus, and God will give him a kingdom that will never end."

Mary almost fainted. "But I'm not married yet," she said.

"Do not worry," said Gabriel. "God will look after you."

Then the angel was gone.

When Mary told Joseph about the angel's message, he was confused. He thought about what Mary had told him, and he decided that he would tell Mary that he could not marry her. That night another angel appeared to Joseph in a dream.

"Do not be afraid," the angel said. "The baby Mary carries is the Son of God. The prophets told of his birth when they said, 'Behold, a virgin shall be with child, and shall bring forth a son, and they shall call his name Emmanuel.'"

Joseph rushed out to tell Mary that he would marry her and help care for Jesus, the Son of God.

So Mary and Joseph were married, and they began to prepare for the coming baby.

One day the emperor, Caesar Augustus, wanted to know how many people were in the Roman Empire. He announced that everybody would return to their family's city to be counted. Since Joseph was from the family of David, he and Mary started out for Bethlehem, David's family home.

When Mary and Joseph arrived in Bethlehem, the streets were crowded with many people who had come to register. Joseph stopped at each inn they saw and asked for a place to stay. But there was no room.

Finally, near the edge of town, they found a stable for shelter. There, along with the animals, Mary and Joseph were at last able to rest.

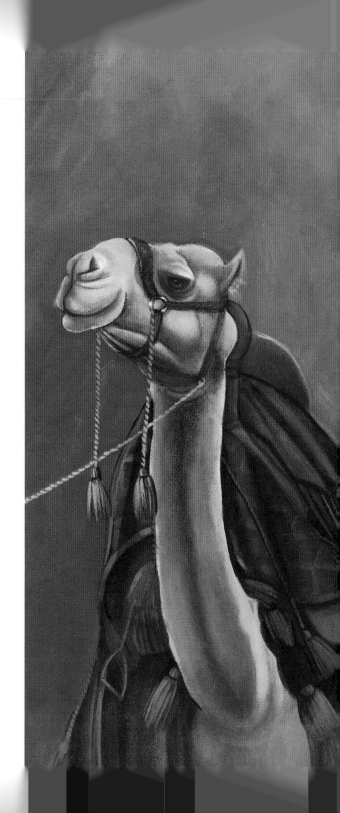

In the soft hay and dim light of the stable, Mary gave birth to her child, the Son of God. She wrapped him in soft cloth and laid him in the straw-filled manger.

"Your name is Jesus, just as the angel said," whispered Mary to her baby.

For hundreds of years, the prophets had spoken of the coming Savior whose kingdom would never end. And on that quiet night in Bethlehem, the prophecies were fulfilled in a tiny baby boy who lay sleeping in a manger.

In the nearby fields, shepherds were watching over their sheep. Suddenly an angel of the Lord appeared before them. They were very frightened.

"Do not be afraid," the angel said, "because I bring you good news. A Savior has been born in Bethlehem. He is Christ the Lord.

"You will find him wrapped in swaddling cloths and lying in a manger."

And suddenly, all around the angel more angels appeared and began praising God and saying, "Glory to God in the highest, and on earth peace, good will to men."

When the angels disappeared, the shepherds said, "Let us go to Bethlehem and see this baby, Christ the Lord!"

They hurried off to find the baby Jesus. When they reached Bethlehem, they found Jesus in the manger, just as the angel had said, and they knelt down and worshiped him.

When the shepherds left, they told everyone about the angel's message and about the baby Jesus.

Far away in the East, wise men lived. They studied the skies and the prophecies.

When Jesus was born, a brilliant star appeared in the sky, and the wise men knew that it marked the birth of a great king. They noted the time and day of the star's appearance, and they set out to find the king.

They went to Jerusalem, to the palace of King Herod. They asked him where they could find the young king. Herod called his chief priests and asked them where the Savior was to be born.

"In Bethlehem of Judea," they told him. The priests read to Herod the words that were written long ago:

"But you, Bethlehem, in the land of Judea, are by no means least among the rulers of Judea; for out of you will come a ruler who will be the shepherd of my people Israel."

Herod and his followers were frightened. Who was this baby who could grow up to be king and take away their leadership?

"Go and make a careful search for the child," Herod said to the wise men. "As soon as you find him, report to me so that I, too, may go and worship him," he lied.

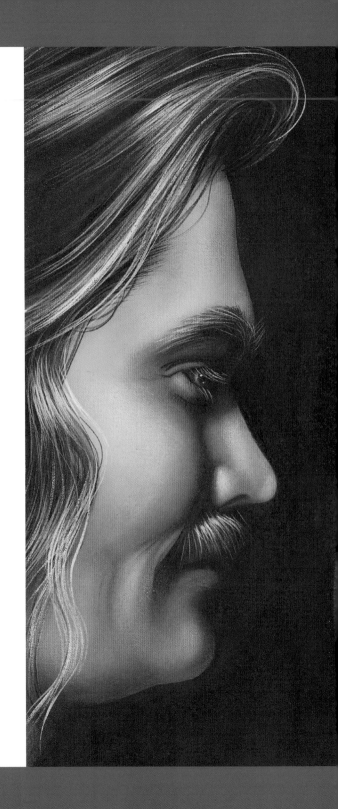

The three wise men gathered their servants and belongings and continued on their journey. They followed the star to Bethlehem.

As they traveled, the star lighted their way. The star stopped over a stable behind an inn. Inside, the wise men found the baby Jesus lying in a manger.

The wise men knelt down and worshiped Jesus. They gave him the gifts they had brought: gold because he was king, frankincense because he was God, and myrrh because Jesus was man.

That night, as the wise men slept, they had a dream that told them not to tell King Herod where to find Jesus. They dreamed that Herod would try to hurt the baby. When the wise men awoke, they left Bethlehem but did not go back to Jerusalem.

When the wise men did not return, King Herod decided to try to find the child.

One night, an angel came to Joseph again in a dream. The angel told him to take Jesus and Mary to Egypt and stay there until it was safe to return.

Joseph, Mary, and Jesus went to Egypt, where they stayed until Herod died. After the death of King Herod, Jesus, Mary, and Joseph returned home to Nazareth.

In Nazareth, Jesus grew up. When he was thirty years old, he began to teach the people about God. People gathered around him wherever he went. Twelve disciples followed him to learn all they could about God and Jesus.

Jesus taught us how to serve God and how to have eternal life. He performed many miracles and healed many people. Through his death and Resurrection, he saved us all.

This is why Christians celebrate Christmas. We remember that Jesus was born to save us and to give us hope. On Christmas morning, we remember the wise men's gifts by giving and receiving presents of our own. And we go to church to honor Jesus and to thank God for sending us his son to give us the gift of everlasting life.